Zebulon Pike: The Life and Legacy of One of Early America's Most Important Explorers

By Charles River Editors

Introduction

David Shankbone's picture of Pikes Peak in Colorado

Throughout his presidency at the beginning of the 19th century, Thomas Jefferson had worried about the future of the western U.S., seeing that settlements in the Ohio Valley and lower South relied upon the Mississippi River. France's controls over the region, in his estimation, put the U.S. at a severe disadvantage. His solution proved successful beyond his wildest imagination, for Napoleon did not only sell New Orleans to the U.S, the portion that Jefferson instructed his ministers to make an offer on, but all of "New France," the entire area of Louisiana. Jefferson might have said later that his purchase of the territory "strained" but did not "break" the Constitution, but also should have boasted that, with one stroke, he had removed one less obstacle to American expansionism.

The Louisiana Purchase encompassed all or part of 15 current U.S. states and two Canadian provinces, including Arkansas, Missouri, Iowa, Oklahoma, Kansas, Nebraska, parts of Minnesota that were west of the Mississippi River, most of North Dakota, nearly all of South Dakota, northeastern New Mexico, Northern Texas, the portions of Montana, Wyoming, and Colorado east of the Continental Divide, and Louisiana west of the Mississippi River, including the city of New Orleans (parts of this area were still claimed by Spain at the time of the Purchase.) In addition, the Louisiana Purchase contained small portions of land that would eventually become part of the Canadian provinces of Alberta and Saskatchewan. The purchase, which doubled the size of the young nation, comprises around 23% of current American territory.

The purchase allowed Jefferson to plan something he had talked about since taking office: an expedition deep into the unmapped and largely unknown continent with the final destination being the Pacific Ocean. This could prove the most significant of the goals that Jefferson - a person who thought of himself as a scientifically-minded thinker - wanted to accomplish as president.[1]

In the aftermath of the Louisiana Purchase, the Lewis and Clark expedition was a much-heralded blow for American rights in the face of international competition, but that was only one of four expeditions authorized by Jefferson. Four years before Lewis and Clark set off, an army officer from New Jersey led two long-distance treks, one northward to the headwaters of the Mississippi River and the other to the Southwest. These were the only expeditions authorized by Jefferson while they were already en route, planned and launched by subordinates within the military.

Given that Lewis and Clark remain so famous, it was inevitable that the other American explorers would be overlooked, particularly William Eaton, the hero of the Battle of Derna in the Barnaby Wars, and Zebulon Montgomery Pike, the explorer of the Mississippi. In the case of Pike, Orsi suggests that the explorer is overlooked and in some cases slighted due to what the expeditions did and did not accomplish. Eaton and Pike represented "the first wave of Manifest Destiny, expanding the republican principles of liberty and citizenship in the world."[2]

Contrasted to that patriotic sentiment are caveats and questions. The career of Zebulon Pike was "dominated by ambiguously motivated explorations of the American West."[3] With the procurement of the Louisiana Purchase, which doubled the size of the nation, Pike had the full force of American authority at his disposal, and his travels through the Colorado Rockies into New Mexico pushed the boundaries between America and Spain. Captured by Spanish officials for illegal entry, he was finally released back into American custody after a year's time with a volume of new information on Spanish territory, its economy, and its military configuration. This sparked a debate about whether the capture was planned by the American government itself.

Pike's return is still debated, as is his relationship with General James Wilkinson and Aaron Burr. The controversy is relevant to Burr's alleged conspiracy to establish a competing empire in the American Southwest, or perhaps as a way of conquering Spanish America without involving the White House. Pike's papers, confiscated by the Spanish, have complicated the search for the

---

[1] " To the Western Ocean: Planning the Lewis and Clark Expedition." Lewis and Clark: The Maps of Exploration 1507-1814 examines. http://www2.lib.virginia.edu/exhibits/lewis_clark/planning.html (accessed November 3, 2012).
[2] Orsi, Jared, Journal of American History
[3] Dedicated Writers, Biography – www.dedicatedwriters.com/biographies/Zebulon-Pike-34961.htm

truth, and any evidence of his complicity remains confidential, in part because of the unpredictable explorer's unpredictable demise.

A Military Boy

Zebulon Montgomery Pike was born on January 5, 1779, in Lamberton, New Jersey, the second of eight children for Zebulon Pike, Sr. and Isabella Pike. Four of Zebulon's siblings died before adulthood, and three others contracted tuberculosis. Little is known of his personal childhood details outside of a passion to visit the banks of the Delaware River, watching it roll by for hours. Pike was born during the American Revolution, and Lamberton is now called Lamington in Bedminster of Somerset County, New Jersey. The community is part of modern Trenton.

He was raised for part of his childhood in Ohio and Illinois in a military environment, and from his experience in numerous army posts, he "absorbed large doses of nationalism."[4] As a child, Zebulon expressed an early intent to achieve public acclaim.

Pike's father was an army colonel who served under General George Washington in the Continental Army during the Revolutionary War. Pike, Sr.'s grandfather (1692-1762) was the first to be named Zebulon, and Pike, Sr.'s great-great-grandfather (1639-1714) served in a company of militia in Woodbridge, New Jersey, in addition to being a judge. John Pike (1613-1689) was the one who initially brought the family to Middlesex. Women in the family were often given the name Zebuline, and the tradition of naming male children Zebulon has continued to this day, with Chief Petty Officer Zebulon Pike serving in the U.S. Navy since 1976.

Pike entered the Army at the age of 15 in 1794 and served under his father's command in the Third United States Infantry. Pike, Sr.'s commander was General James Wilkinson (1757-1825), who would become an important figure in Pike's later career. The elder Pike had previously left the army and attempted to make a living in retirement as a farmer, but he and Isabella were never able to reach personal independence, struggling to pay taxes and holding on to their land. As a result, he had reluctantly rejoined the army in 1791.

---

[4] Encyclopedia.com, Zebulon Montgomery Pike – www.encyclopedia.com

Wilkinson

Pike, Sr. began his career in public life as "an ardent Federalist"[5] and was involved in the high-profile public whipping of a Republican newspaper editor at Reading, Pennsylvania on June 24, 1779 as a member of the military. By some means or other, he escaped punishment, and he ultimately passed along his political passions to his son.

In 1796, with the United States maintaining a tenuous hold on the northern borders, General Georges Henri Victor Collot, a French officer, was tasked with touring the Mississippi River to the north. He was instructed to draw maps in case France found the opportunity to seize the territory away from the "nascent"[6] United States. The 17-year-old Zebulon Pike shadowed Collot's party a good distance up the river. Even though America claimed the north, the French government, Collot, and others suspected that they could locate a good number of settlers with sympathies to France. Pike's participation in tracking Collot was no childish exercise or prank, for Pike had already served for two years and was to become a commissioned officer by the age

---

[5] Cutrer, Thomas, TSHA, Texas State Historical Association, Pike, Zebulon Montgomery (1779-1813) – www.tshaonline.org/handbook/entries/pike-zebulon-montgomery/

[6] Celebnetworth, Biography and Timeline, Zebulon Montgomery Pike – www.celebnetworth.com/zebulon-pike/

of 20.

Pike, like his father, went on to serve under General "Mad Anthony" Wayne, who earned his nickname for bravery and quick temper. Under Wayne's command, Pike ferried supplies along the Miami River, gaining "valuable experience in supervision"[7] and as an agent for private contractors who supplied the army with food, clothing, and other provisions. In a more active role, Pike participated in raids against the various native tribes residing in the Ohio Valley.

Wayne

Zebulon's father, now Captain Pike, Sr., was in frequent contact with General Wayne, telling him of recent events affecting the western parts of the Northwest Territory, including his "troubles with deserters and a Lieutenant Gregg."[8] Another difficulty Pike explained was that of "the Spanish colonial government's preparations for war with the United States,"[9] and their

---

[7] Encyclopedia.com

[8] Indiana Historical Society, We Do History, June 8, 1796 – www.images.indianahistory.org/digital/collection/ONWT/id/1658/

[9] Indiana Historical Society

"encouragement of deserters and others to move to the west side of the Mississippi River."[10] His son's tracking of Collot's movements assisted Pike in sending these reports to Wayne.

In 1798, young Zebulon was transferred to what was then the country's southwestern frontier. He served as Thomas Jefferson's personal representative for three years as commissioner, negotiating with the natives to allow the building of more military posts. Pike noted the reluctance of the natives to sell their land but continued the mission to "move Indian populations around in [an] agrarian economy."[11]

Pike repeatedly visited an old friend of his father, Captain John Alston Brown, presumably as a man of possible influence to the progression of his career. However, he also grew smitten by Brown's daughter, Clarissa Harlow Brown, who was 18, and the affection was requited. Captain Brown had strong objections to his daughter marrying a soldier, particularly one whose future career was speculative. As he put it, "A soldier for my daughter's hand, sir? I cannot agree with it."[12] Neither side of the family made much mention of the fact that Captain Brown was Isabella Pike's brother, making the couple first cousins.

Despite the probability of a financial carrot extended by Clarissa's father to break it off, Pike and Clarissa eloped in Cincinnati in 1801, a daring social statement for such an era. However, it was a time in which revolution and cries for freedom had been promoted in both hemispheres well before the American Revolution, and the next generation after that war was affected by it.

No one was more prepared to employ the new rhetoric of revolution than Zebulon Pike. In a letter to his father shortly after his marriage, he employed the Greek-style feint of quasi-apology before boldly stating his position. To his father, Pike began with the admission that "my conduct…may possibly be a little independent,"[13] but he then fell back at once on the sentiments of Jefferson and Thomas Paine: "Nothing can justify an unconditional submission to the will of any man…should I be confined to the walls of a prison still shall my heart be free."[14] Only one of the couple's children survived to adulthood. Their daughter, Clarissa Brown Pike went on to marry the son of William Henry Harrison.

Life on the Ohio frontier was far from comfortable. Pain, hunger, boredom, illness, extreme temperatures, insecurity, and other miseries "afflicted them relentlessly."[15] Pike practiced hard labor to get by, and the strain was worse on Pike's parents. By his early 50s, his father was a broken man, no longer fit for command.

---

[10] Indiana Historical Society

[11] Indiana Historical Society

[12] Jared Orsi, Zebulon Pike and his "Frozen Lands, Bodies, Nationalism, and the West in the Early Republic, *Western Historical Quarterly,* Vol. 42 No. 1 (Spring 2011)

[13] Jared Orsi, Western Historical Quarterly

[14] Jared Orsi, Western Historical Quarterly

[15] Jared Orsi, Western Historical Quarterly

Pike had always felt a sense of shame over his lack of formal education. With that in mind, he began a regimen of "self-education by candlelight."[16] Even on duty, he could be seen "carrying books into the wilderness and reading voluminously."[17] In a constant search for self-improvement, by the time of his first officer promotion, he had taught himself French and mathematics and over time had become "a tolerable English scholar."[18]

Pike also eventually turned his attention to "scientific improvement."[19] Among his most influential readings was Robert Dodsley's *The Economy of Human Life,* and to balance out his curriculum, he read Alexander Pope and Samuel Johnson. Of particular interest to some scholars is that Pike published a "curious little book"[20] that he purported to be a translation of the *Tibetan Book of Wisdom*. His regimen went from a rudimentary rural school status for the day to fluency in French, Spanish, and considerably sophisticated English.

To go with his expanding education, Pike was described as a "slim, blue-eyed pompous young man with an odd habit of tilting his head to one side."[21] He was 5'8, "tolerably square and robust…his complexion was then ruddy, eyes blue, light hair and good features…gentlemanly, agreeable and polished."[22]

The Journey North

Pike was assigned a position in logistics and payroll at Fort Kaskaskia, Illinois, on the banks of the Mississippi River, and it was there that Pike caught the attention of Wilkinson, who was now the Governor of Upper Louisiana Territory in St. Louis. In short order, Pike "became his protégé."[23]

In 1805, Pike was stationed at Fort Belle Fontaine, the first American military installation west of the Mississippi River. Built in that year under the leadership of Lieutenant Colonel Jacob Kingsbury, Belle Fontaine became an important gathering spot for officers, enlisted men, native groups, French, Spanish, and American settlers, alongside trappers and traders. It included a factory and eventually 30 buildings with several blockhouses and an arsenal. Today it is a 350-acre park.

---

[16] Jared Orsi, Western Historical Quarterly

[17] Jared Orsi, Western Historical Quarterly

[18] Jared Orsi, Western Historical Quarterly

[19] Jared Orsi, Western Historical Quarterly

[20] Jared Orsi, Western Historical Quarterly

[21] Jared Orsi, Western Historical Quarterly

[22] Jared Orsi, Western Historical Quarterly

[23] Our Iowa Heritage, Zebulon Pike and his 'Dam'd Rascals' – www.ouriowaheritage.com/our-iowa-heritage-zebulon-pike/

A picture of the fort's ruins

Under the watchful eye of General Wilkinson, Pike was handpicked for two noteworthy expeditions, the first to the north and the other to the Southwest. Several biographers have noted how strange it was that Wilkinson chose an officer who had already been stationed at numerous forts without any spectacular feats to show for it. Of course, these kinds of expeditions were precisely the kinds of feats that could bring the public acclaim Pike most craved.

Wilkinson had been born in Calvert County, Maryland, and he served as a medical doctor, American soldier and adventurer, and ultimately a "double agent"[24] with Spain. His role in the infamous Aaron Burr conspiracy "still divides historians."[25] He served in the American Revolution and settled in Kentucky, but in 1787 he took a secret oath of allegiance to Spain despite being an American official. He was also active in the movement for Kentucky statehood. Through the end of the 18th century, Wilkinson received a pension from Spain, known only as "Number 13." As a double agent, he once took a payment of $12,000 from Spain for delivering a fake American invasion plan.

As a former protégé of Benedict Arnold during the Revolution, Wilkinson was behooved to exercise caution. He had already been court-martialed a decade earlier for a letter-writing

---

²⁴ Britannica, James Wilkinson – www.britannica.com/biography/James-Wilkinson
²⁵ Britannica, Wilkinson

campaign designed to discredit General Wayne, who was chosen over him for the post of Commanding General. Everyone along the chain of command was aware of Wilkinson's vanity and believed that promoting him to Brigadier General would alleviate the situation. Ironically, when Spanish agents were caught in the act of transporting payments to him, Wayne attempted to have him court-martialed, but Wayne died of a stomach disorder in 1796 before the proceedings got underway, and Wilkinson was acquitted. As a result, the double agent was still along the frontier and perfectly positioned to cause problems.

As Governor of the Louisiana Purchase above the 33rd parallel, Wilkinson attempted to realize his ambition to conquer the Mexican provinces of Spain and perhaps set up an independent government. It is possible that these ambitions were in mind when he sent Pike on two expeditions, the first up the Mississippi River to its headwaters and the second to Colorado, skirting and probing Spanish territory. No proof has ever come to light that Pike was aware of Wilkinson's actual machinations, but the possibility has been debated for about 200 years.

The "official" goal of the first expedition may have been to pinpoint the location of Mississippi's headwaters, but there were other motivations, official and unofficial. Surveying and acquiring native lands on which to build military forts and outposts took priority, so the American officials in the area were supposed to hold "peace talks" with important native chiefs.

For his part, Pike relished the third aspect of the mission: to "confront any British soldiers and/or Canadian fur traders for violations of treaty and international protocol associated with the Louisiana Purchase."[26]

With these goals, Lieutenant Pike led a 20-man party up the Mississippi to negotiate peace and assert the legal claim of the United States to anyone then living within American borders. Pike and his men departed from Belle Fontaine on August 9, 1805.

On September 21, Pike was on the island that now bears his name. He purchased 100,000 acres of land from the Dakota Sioux for 60 gallons of liquor. This was fortunate for Pike, as he was not authorized to make cash transactions on behalf of the government.

On September 22, at the mouth of Peter's River, Pike met with Sioux Chief Petit Corbeau and 150 of his Sioux warriors. The expedition team was met with a standard salutation in the native manner. Some had never seen a white man, but one who had encountered them from all sorts of countries observed upon meeting Pike, "The American is neither a Frenchman nor an Englishman, but a white Indian."[27]

For centuries, the natives had "created a complex culture in the Mississippi Valley,"[28] using the

---

[26] Britannica, Wilkinson

[27] Marco Soli, When the Mississippi Was an Indian River, University of Michigan, *Revue français d'études américaine*, Dec. 2003, No. 98, Stemming the Mississippi

trade of maize for the development of society. The largest city, centuries before the white man's arrival, was Cahokia, which was near contemporary St. Louis and had 20,000 inhabitants at its peak.

By the time winter set in, Pike's men had reached a spot 100 miles north of the Falls of St. Anthony. Getting the boat around the falls was extremely difficult, and Pike "drove his men so hard that seven became ill and the rest dropped from exhaustion."[29] The sergeant was vomiting blood. The 70-foot keelboat had to be hauled by a party of only 20, and the falls were circumvented after much effort. Likewise, it had to be dragged over sand bars on a regular basis, and Pike was not a patient man.

Of the men who departed St. Louis, the main body stayed a day or two behind "hauling supplies on sleds,"[30] stopping regularly to "set fires for the others."[31] Pike was unaware that Lake Itasca was the original source of the river 30 miles to the east. The party visited several British fur posts along the way, continuing upstream along the frozen river on foot. Once they reached Little Falls, the small party went on to Leech Lake on February 1, 1806. Wintering with the Sioux at Little Falls, the party spent a few harsh months, but they were not unproductive ones, as Pike was able to arrange a treaty and to map much of the region.

Wilkinson, despite sponsoring the expedition, did not think to include a doctor or an interpreter with the group, and even now, it's hard to imagine anyone in 1805 thinking that a doctor would not be required on such an arduous journey. Moreover, Pike was given antique equipment for determining the latitude, a watch, and a thermometer. Wilkinson did not forget to send a pack of hunting dogs and whiskey for bartering, and the federal government officially spent $2,000 equipping the crew. As for translation, Pike was often at a loss for how to communicate with the chiefs.

Mistaking Leech Lake as the Mississippi River's source was an easy conclusion to reach. At a distance of over 30 miles to the west of Grand Rapids, during the wet season Leech Lake is capable of supplying a greater quantity of water to the Upper Mississippi than any of the other northern sources. Pike was aware of Lake Itasca, the true headwaters of the river, but it's understandable that he did not recognize that was the source during the winter season.

The expedition spent three weeks at Leech Lake and the Sandy Lakes. Pike set about informing all area residents that they were now living under American law. He made it clear to the Ojibwe and Dakota that they were to cease all mutual hostilities, and his crew unceremoniously began

---

[28] W.E. Hollon

[29] Midwestern Weekends, Pike on the Prowl, For Better or Worse, America's First Emissary on the Upper Mississippi Set History into Motion, Dec. 1, 2020 – www.midwesternweekends.com/plan-a-trip/history-heritage/frontier-history/zebulon-pike/

[30] Biography, Zebulon Pike. Your Dictionary – www.biography.yourdictionary.com/zebulon-pike

[31] Hollon, W.E., Zebulon Montgomery Pike and the Wilkinson-Burr Conspiracy, Proceedings of the *American Philosophical Society,* Dec. 3, 1947, Vol. 91, no. 4

shooting down the Union Jack wherever they saw it being flown, raising an American one in its place.

On the northward trip, the expedition spent 23 days in the land that was to become Iowa, the "Beautiful Land," as it was called by residents. On the return trip, they spent 11 days. There, they met with Julien Dubuque, a French fur trader working in the area, but every attempt to make conversation with Dubuque was met with either silence or incomprehensible evasion. Pike only asked for standard information on that area, but cooperation was not forthcoming. It turned out that Dubuque had signed a deal with the Spanish to work the lead mines near Catfish Creek, and he could not be certain that the Americans would allow him to keep control of that land given to him by the Spanish.

Along the way, Pike mapped many Mississippi tributaries. The states of Wisconsin and Illinois were first settled based on some of these maps. At McGregor, Iowa, Pike correctly assessed that the bluffs overlooking the river would make an excellent fort location. However, his recommendation was rejected, and a fort was built in the Mississippi floodplain instead. The entire company in residence at the new fort was forced to move three times due to flooding.

Stopping at a group of islands on their return, Pike's men found hundreds of nesting passenger pigeons there, and he brought nearly 300 of them aboard. They killed many of the young, and according to Pike, the noise was "like the continued roaring of the wind."[32] Early writers of natural history cite few known nesting sites for passenger pigeons as of 1806, but the event contradicts Hollon's idea that Pike never interacted with nature. No one has offered any explanation for the fates of the pigeons, namely whether they were released, domesticated, or eaten.

Pike, according to those who worked with him and served under him, was personally quirky and often unpredictable. Though brave and patriotic, he still had a penchant for blundering. It is said that he "blithely mistreated his men and their British hosts"[33] on the Mississippi journey, and National Forest Service Ranger and historian David Wiggins quipped, "He's no Lewis and Clark…sometimes I call him the B-Squad Lewis and Clark."[34] With a longing to be included in the elitist group, "he liked being anointed into the ranks of Lewis and Clark. He was a puffed-up little popinjay who had all these pretensions to greatness."[35]

Poised as he was socially, he was also famous for his "fits of pique."[36] After signing a treaty with one of the native tribes, he discovered that his flag was missing and had "a tantrum, beating

---

[32] Jimmy L. Bryan, Unquestionable Geographies, *Pacific Historical Review*, Fall 2018, Vol.; 87 No.4

[33] David Wiggins, National Forest Service Forest Ranger, Midwestern Weekends - www.midwesternweekends.com/plan-a-trip/history-heritage/frontier-history/zebulon-pike/

[34] David Wiggins, Midwest Weekends

[35] David Wiggins, Midwest Weekends

[36] David Wiggins, Midwest Weekends

one of his soldiers in front of the Lakota."[37] On the following day, it was found floating 15 miles downstream. Once notified, he sent men on a 30-mile round trip hike to fetch it.

On another occasion, he fashioned a dugout canoe that immediately sank "with all his stuff, and his special black gunpowder g[ot] wet."[38] He ordered the men to dry out the powder over the fire, and it naturally caught fire, "explode[d], and burn[ed] up his tent."[39] In a modern context, Pike has been likened by Wiggins to the character of Major Frank Burns in the television series *MASH*, though Wiggins also pointed out that Burns would have "wimped out"[40] early. Park Naturalist Linda Radimecky agreed, acknowledging that Pike "had the stamina of an ox."[41]

John Anfinson, a National Park Service historian, explained that after enjoying British hospitality at one of the fur company's outposts for 10 days, even borrowing the clothes of the British proprietor after his legs became overly swollen, Pike repaid the favor by hoisting the American flag and "having his men shoot down the Union Jack."[42] Anfison noted, "What I don't understand is why they didn't just shoot Pike and be done with it, because he was so in their face about it."[43] He further added that Pike was a "pompous teetotaler"[44] who hid in the bushes to catch his men drinking. At the same time, Anfinson conceded that Pike was an excellent hunter who often provided for all his men singlehandedly.[45]

All in all, the expedition up the Mississippi and back lasted for 264 days and covered more than 2,000 miles, passing through five of today's states. Pike managed to purchase the land on which Minneapolis and St. Paul currently are located, and for the new government's purposes, "exploration and consolidation went hand in hand"[46] in terms of reinforcing American law in the newly acquired lands. The expanding national boundaries were enforced in a way that would be seen by international competitors as resolute. In this area, Pike saw himself as "a champion of nation-building in an era of fragile national allegiances almost everywhere."[47]

However, in the end, at least one historian described the accomplishments of the Mississippi River expedition as "disappointingly meager."[48] W.E. Hollon noted that while Pike's failure to reach the headwaters by a mere 25 miles was not the end of the world, Pike's gestures toward the British North West Fur Company proved to be futile, and foreign trappers and traders continued to violate American law with impunity. Nearly all of the native groups at war with one another

---

[37] David Wiggins, Midwest Weekends

[38] David Wiggins, Midwest Weekends

[39] David Wiggins, Midwest Weekends

[40] David Wiggins, Midwest Weekends

[41] Linda Radimecky, Midwest Weekends

[42] John Anfinson, Midwest Weekends

[43] John Anfinson, Midwest Weekends

[44] John Anfinson, Midwest Weekends

[45] John Anfinson, Midwest Weekends

[46] Jared Orsi, The Life of Zebulon Pike, Review by Stephen Aron, *Book Reviews*, UCLA

[47] Jared Orsi, Stephen Aron

[48] W.E. Hollon

continued their hostilities the moment Pike was out of earshot, particularly the Chippewa and the Sioux. Added to that was Britain's success in allying with nearly every native group in the region, which would be crucial for the subsequent War of 1812.

In the wake of Pike's journey, not a single chief accepted the "invitation" to meet with Wilkinson in St. Louis, little if any scientific knowledge was gained, and Pike "did not locate a single stream or lake that had not been previously discovered and named."[49] No plants or animals of the regions traveled through were brought back or sent back to satisfy Jefferson's scientific curiosity. No natural history specimens were collected at all. Put simply, nothing was described or catalogued, and the maps, poorly drawn, ended up being "inaccurate as to latitude, distances, and directions."[50] Modern historians are aware that Pike's journals contain "many obvious errors and contradictions. It is badly arranged, and difficult to follow."[51] To his credit, the expedition did focus attention on the boundaries for Canada and the Louisiana Purchase, but there was little else for Pike to truly hang his hat on.[52]

At the root of it, Wilkinson likely cared little about whether the true source of the Mississippi was correctly determined. Indeed, the exclusion of a doctor or interpreter suggests that the announced goals were not his true motives. Historians have since speculated that Wilkinson was aiming to provoke the British, who controlled Canada at the time, by sending an official American expedition to the border. Given what is now known, it's altogether possible Wilkinson's "dubious loyalties"[53] provided the impetus for the expedition.

The Journey South

The promotion of Pike's Mississippi expedition was "clumsily put together for the press but managed to capture the imagination of a large segment of the American public…curious about the West."[54] Thus, once the Mississippi party had returned, Wilkinson wasted no time before sending Pike and his company out again. In less than three months, they were to be outfitted for a journey that would traverse several thousand miles to what is now the American Southwest.

In 1806, America experienced a "year of expansionist fever."[55] Oregon Country had been made famous by Lewis and Clark but was coveted by the British, while the Russians occupied much of the far north. To the Southwest lay the Spanish territories, but Spain was involved militarily elsewhere, and Spain's attempt to manage an increasingly discontented Mexican independence movement proved burdensome.

---

[49] W.E. Hollon

[50] W.E. Hollon

[51] W.E. Hollon

[52] W.E. Hollon

[53] Robert McNamara, Thought Co, Zebulon Pike's Mysterious, Western Expeditions: Mysterious Motives Remain Puzzling to This Day, 2/2/2019 – www.thoughtco.com/zebulon-pike-led-two-expeditions-1773817

[54] Biography, Zebulon Pike

[55] Biography, Zebulon Pike

Wilkinson's instructions for Pike's Southwest expedition sounded innocent enough, but he was also likely told to find a secret route to the Spanish settlement of Santa Fe, the capital of the Spanish province. "Ripe for trading with the outside world, New Spain pursued a strict isolationist policy and dealt firmly with trespassing neighbors."[56] Many Americans wanted to get their hands on Spanish silver coins, but when caught, their goods were confiscated and they were expelled.

Spain had a weak military presence in the Southwest and was concerned about American expansion. Fearing their inability to protect such vast land holdings, Spanish orders from Mexico were to "keep imperial borders closed to foreigners, especially foreign trade."[57] All trade was conducted deep in Mexico, making manufactured goods "costly and scarce."[58] The region was so sealed off that the people had no knowledge of their new American neighbor. Americans, on the other hand, would be excited to hear that one of their own explorers had broken the barriers and lived to tell of it.

Pike and his expedition sailed on July 15, 1806, from Belle Fontaine Landing in two boats. Aboard were two lieutenants, a surgeon, a sergeant, two corporals, 16 privates, and an interpreter named Baronet Vasquez (called Bernie by friends). The presence of a doctor and interpreter must have been a welcome change for Pike.

On board as well for the first leg of the journey were chiefs of the Osage and Pawnee tribes, with a number of women and children. They had recently visited Jefferson in Washington and were redeemed from being held captive by the Potowatomies. Pike was instructed to return these 51 people to their home among the Osages.

The company's departure from the confluence of the Mississippi and the Missouri included General James Wilkinson's son, Lieutenant B. Wilkinson, and the "ever interesting"[59] and mysterious Dr. John Hamilton Robinson, added as a "volunteer surgeon."[60] Robinson was touted as having a "good shooting eye,"[61] and Pike described him as the "right arm of the expedition."[62] Otherwise, no one understood why he was part of the team.

Robinson was a self-adventurer, an explorer, a spy, and a former physician in St. Louis. He served as the State Department emissary to New Spain for three years, at the same time urging Americans to take up arms and overthrow Spanish rule. Pike was an "old companion"[63] of

---

[56] When America Was Young, Zebulon Pike and the Santa Fe Trail – www.whenamericawasyoung.com/pike-santa-fe-trail

[57] World History US, Zebulon Pike to Santa Fe, July 4, 2017 – www.worldhistory.org/american-history-the-great-american-plains/zebulon-pike-to-santa-fe.php

[58] World History

[59] Santa Fe Trail Research, Zebulon Pike's Expedition to the Southwest-1807 – www.santafetrailresearch.com/pike/expedition.htm

[60] Santa Fe Trail Research,

[61] Jackson, Donald, *American Heritage Foundation*, The Question Is: How Lost Was Zebulon Pike? Feb. 1965, Vol. 16 No. 2

[62] Jackson, Donald

[63] David Narrett, Liberation and Conquest: John Hamilton Robinson and U.S. Adventurism toward Mexico, 1806-1819, *Western Historical*

Robinson and agreed that "20,000 U.S. auxiliaries"[64] and Mexican revolutionaries should be sufficient to overthrow the Spanish, who were technically still at peace with America.

Robinson was a "confidence man"[65] recommended by Wilkinson to "shore up an inexperienced Pike,"[66] and as one dealing in his own brand of subterfuge once reaching Northern New Spain. He became famous for his declaration, "Europe enslaved millions! America liberated them!"[67] At the same time, it would be Robinson who, when taken to Mexico for questioning after this expedition was intercepted, slipped the Spanish officials a confidential note offering to become a Spanish subject and lead a royal expedition to the Pacific coast.

Indeed, before Pike even departed from St. Louis, Spanish spies in the United States were rushing word of a proposed march on Chihuahua, where Nemesio de Salcedo maintained his headquarters. This rumor was likely a false invasion plan peddled by Wilkinson to the Spanish, but regardless, Salcedo ordered a force of cavalry under Don Facundo Melgares to move north, pick up native allies, and stop Pike, even within the confines of the Louisiana Purchase if necessary.

Pike successfully reached the Osage and Pawnee tribal grounds, so Chevaux Blanche (White Hair) and Sans Oreille (No Ears) were returned to their homes, but not without some show of pomp and machismo. Three miles from the village, Pike wrote, "We were requested to remain."[68] The Pawnee advanced on Pike's party and "came on like a real war charge."[69] Pike described how the warriors encircled his party until the chief, named Caracterish, advanced in the center and offered his hand. The expedition spent several weeks with the Pawnee.

Ironically, the force of Mexican soldiers sent out by Salcedo to turn Pike back had arrived a few days earlier at some of the native villages. The Spanish in the New Mexico Territory had been alarmed by American plans when Jefferson sent out Lewis and Clark, and now they were doubly alarmed. When Pike arrived in the area, one of the first things he saw was the Spanish flag flying overhead, on orders of Don Facundo Melgares. It bothered Pike to the point where he spent most of his negotiating time persuading the Pawnee to take down Melgares' flag. Eventually, the Pawnee complied, even offering a guarantee that they would cease trade with the Spanish. However, the Spanish had instructed the Pawnee not to allow Pike to travel any further west. It took a good deal of hard negotiating to leave the village, after which the expedition continued in a westward direction.

In the coming decades, the Cherokee would plead with the government for protection from the

---

[64] David Narrett
[65] David Narrett
[66] David Narrett
[67] David Narrett
[68] Santa Fe Trail Research
[69] Santa Fe Trail Research

Osages, who continued their warlike behavior after Pike departed. They reminded the government that they had undergone a forced march decades ago to a new home they did not choose and were promised protection upon their arrival.

Pike's next order of business was a daunting attempt to "proselytize the Comanche."[70] Around October 15, the party reached Cheyenne Bottom to the northeast of Great Bend, Kansas, and by November 23, they were in Pueblo, where they first sighted the mountain later to be known as Pikes Peak, at first nothing more than a small blue cloud on the distant horizon 150 miles away. He had no idea that the mountain stood at 14,110 feet, not the tallest mountain in America, but vastly more prodigious than anything to be found east of the Mississippi.

Three decades earlier, Juan Bautista de Anza, Governor of New Mexico, had led 800 soldiers with Ute and Apache allies against the Comanche into the area known as Manitou Springs. It is unknown whether he or any among his army attempted to summit the mountain, and if not, Pike was the first white man to try it. However, reaching it took four months, and Pike initially believed that the entire expedition would be complete within six months.

The undertaking of climbing Pikes Peak was an "ill-advised attempt."[71] The men were entirely unprepared for winter and climbed in "thin cotton uniforms"[72] through deep snow and sub-zero temperatures. The party never reached the mountain per se and probably scaled Mt. Cheyenne or Mt. Rosa thinking it would lead to the summit of the larger peak. Pike ultimately abandoned the climb and pronounced that the mountain was unclimbable. Stephen Long's expedition, more appropriately dressed for the occasion, reached the summit 14 years later.

Pikes Peak took on tremendous symbolic value from that day on. Katharine Lee Bates deemed Pikes Peak to be "America's Mountain."[73] It was formerly named Tava ("sun" in the Ute language), Heey-otoyoo ("Long Mountain" in the Arapaho language), and El Capitán (in Spanish). Bates wrote the poem that would become the lyrics for *America the Beautiful*, which was originally entitled *Pikes Peak*. The music was composed by Samuel A. Ward, a New Jersey church organist, and published as *America the Beautiful*.

After the first crossing of the Great Plains to the Southwest, Pike opined that the barren stretch would forever be a means for white settlers to reach the Pacific states, but that no white person would ever consider living there. While some explorers in the wet season characterized the mystery of the Great Plains in terms of its potential, Eastern writers who were anti-expansion turned it into a horror story. It was promoted as a desert much like the Sahara and nothing more than a barrier to western movement toward the fertile coastal valleys. Jefferson took the more optimistic view, observing that the Great Plains were likely treeless because the "soil was too

---

[70] Donald Jackson, American Heritage

[71] History, This Day in History, April 17, 1813 – www.history.com/this-day-in-history/explorer-zebulon-ike-dies

[72] History

[73] History of Pike's Peak – www.pikespeak.us.com/learn-history-of-pikes-peak

rich."[74] Pike did not share Jefferson's penchant for rationalization, claiming that "the vast plain of the western hemisphere may become in time equally celebrated as the sandy deserts in Africa."[75] Despite his doubts that anyone would settle there, he was correct that the Great Plains would see an enormous westward flow of settlers, with "our citizens being so prone to rambling and extending themselves on the frontiers."[76]

Having moved from the Osage villages to Pueblo to the west, the party's movements became erratic. Turning into South Park from Cañon City, through Buena Vista and back into the Arkansas watershed created a disorienting detour as they stumbled down the Royal Gorge of Colorado. Moving in a circle, they came out again at the Arkansas River.

Inexplicably moving toward Spanish territory with a crossing of the Sangre de Cristo Mountains, they went without food for several days on a couple of occasions. The expedition struggled across "one of the passes above what is now the Great Sand Dunes National Park and Preserve."[77] At one point, Pike realized that his party was in serious trouble, but it was too late to turn back. He was forced to leave five men behind with all the horses. Several of the men contracted gangrene, and their feet had to be amputated.

In early February, Pike hunkered down and built a stockade on the Conejos River, a tributary of the Rio Grande. It was not a grand structure, but a simple shelter of cottonwood trees. Dr. Robinson "begged leave to contact Spanish officials in Santa Fe"[78] and collect a debt from an Illinois merchant. He produced a document for the governor in Santa Fe giving him the authority to collect an overdue sum from Kaskaskia. On that trip, Robinson told the governor that he had recently left a party of hunters in the mountains that were in serious trouble. Alarmed by the report, the Spanish sent out a large patrol to apprehend them.

The expedition had become lost steering itself toward Spanish land, but it is historically difficult to determine how much of Pike's claims of being lost are true. He expressed a hope that "the Spanish would capture him so that he could see more of the territory."[79] If so, his gamble certainly paid off. Either way, Pike was apparently not surprised when 100 Spanish Mexican dragoons and militiamen appeared at the gate of his stockade. When informed he was on Spanish land, he argued that the Red River was on the American side. When the Spaniards responded that he was for all intents and purposes on the Rio Grande River, and that he was under arrest for illegal entry, he cheerfully lowered the American flag over his "fort" and was escorted away.

Some sources characterize Pike's crude shelter as a fortification, as if to heighten a

---

[74] Kevin Z. Sweeney, Wither the Fruited Plain: The Long Expedition and the Description of the "Great American Desert," *Great Plains Quarterly* Vol. 25 No. 2 (Spring 2005), University of Nebraska

[75] Kevin Z. Sweeney

[76] Thomas Cutrer, THSA

[77] Jared Orsi, Zebulon Montgomery Pike, Colorado Encyclopedia – www.coloradoencyclopedia/article/zebulon-montgomery-pike

[78] Legends of America, Zebulon Pike, Hard-Luck Soldier & Explorer – www.legendsofamerica.com/we-zebulonpike/

[79] Jared Orsi

confrontation with the Spaniards, but it was no more than a four-sided windbreak, more for defense against the natives than Spanish soldiers. It was not a "fortification."[80] Those who claim otherwise are said to be promoting the idea that Pike was in league with the Burr conspiracy. The only special feature of the shelter was a few portholes and a moat surrounding it.

Through it all, Pike only lost one man. William Meek was apparently murdered by a native, but even that has been contradicted by alternate evidence. It may be that Meek killed Private Theodore Miller during a drunken argument and was imprisoned in Mexico until 1821.

The Spanish confiscated all of Pike's journals and papers, only to be recovered more than 100 years later by Herbert Eugene Bolton from the Mexican government archives. He published them in the *American Historical Review* in 1908, and they now reside in the Archives Division of the Adjutant General's Office. Pike was able to hide some papers in his men's gun barrels.

During their captivity, the men were all treated well, indicative of the fact that, uneasy as the relationship between Spain and the U.S. may have been, they were not at war. Pike noticed at once how thinly the Spanish military was spread from a separate conflict against Napoleon's brother across the Atlantic.

Pike had promised to send rescue parties back to gather up the men who were left behind. Once that was complete, he was taken to the governor in Santa Fe. Along the way, he enjoyed parties and conversations with both Spanish priests and officials, gathering a considerable body of information on the region's geography, population, economy, and military defenses. He was "wined and dined" by the priests, and he was entertained by troupes of Spanish ladies, courtesy of the officials.

Although Pike's men were never mistreated, they were separated from each other at all times, and after they were released, Salcedo was reprimanded by his government for doing so. Spain had heard of the Lewis and Clark expedition,[81] and Salcedo's orders were to "terminate all such expeditions into disputed territory."[82]

The accusation persists that Pike was "never truly lost," and that he concocted the whole story for the Spanish. He certainly knew that there was no Red River as far west as the Rocky Mountains, as it runs through the high plains of New Mexico. His excuse for being on the Rio Grande was either a "long-planned lie,"[83] or his geographical sense did not suit him for the explorer's life at all. Once returned, he published his letter to Wilkinson as proof he was truly lost. "He believed that the reading public would believe so, too."[84]

---

[80] Carter, Carroll Joe, Pike in Colorado, Review by Maxine Benson, Adams State College, Alamosa

[81] Donald Jackson, American Heritage

[82] Donald Jackson, American Heritage

[83] Donald Jackson, American Heritage

[84] Donald Jackson, American Heritage

With that said, when he realized that he had miscalculated locations, he scratched corrections into his journal like someone who realized his mistakes. The Arkansas became the Red River, and the Red River became the "Rio del Nord." To historian Donald Jackson, this reveals that Pike was indeed lost, "not once, but twice."[85]

For Pike, reputation meant everything. No matter how ambitious he was, determined not to duplicate his father's "drab" career, "now poor, lame, and occasionally addled,"[86] he would have found being the object of scandal equally unbearable.

By the same token, Pike was never above legal scheming, and although far more scrupulous than Wilkinson, he sought out patronage shamelessly. He wrote to his father, pleading to receive "closed letters…to any friends of influence you may have. I have schemes in view that require every exertion in my power to accomplish."[87] The power of influence held by Captain Pike, Sr.'s professional circle is likely dubious at best, with most having retired. Regardless, his son was an ambitious man, "a born protégé, waiting for a patron."[88]

With a sense of elitism, Pike desired that the Army maintain itself as an intimate unit manned by a small group of aristocrats, self-appointed or otherwise. Pike remained outspoken about the "democratization of the army during the Thomas Jefferson administration."[89] He was one of three Federalists to accept promotion and transfer into a new regiment when Jefferson expanded the army in 1807.

While in Spanish captivity, Pike purchased two grizzly bear cubs and shipped them across the country to Jefferson in a moment of poor foresight, as it demonstrated the lax sort of captivity he suffered. The soldiers carried the two cubs on their laps as they rode mules. Instead of bear milk, they were fed on corn mush. During a pause, the men built a cage of branches and lashed it to two mules.

The bears arrived safely in New Orleans, where they were transferred to the merchant ship, *Neptune*, bound for the White House via Baltimore Harbor. Accompanying them was a "box of pecans."[90] Jefferson was fond of the pecans, but somewhat "less enamored of the bears."[91] Already too big to have ambling on the White House grounds, he handed them over to Charles Wilson Peale, founder of the Philadelphia Museum. Peale housed thousands of natural history specimens, and he "wanted the works of man and nature to coexist for the edification of all."[92]

---

[85] Donald Jackson, American Heritage

[86] Donald Jackson, American Heritage

[87] Donald Jackson, American Heritage

[88] Donald Jackson, American Heritage

[89] Thomas Cutrer, TSHA

[90] Wise, Michael D., Seeing Like a Stomach: Food, the Body, and Jeffersonian Exploration in the Near Southwest, Southwestern Historical *Quarterly* Vol. 120 No. 4 (April 2017)

[91] Michael D. Wise

[92] Karie Diethorn, Peale's Philadelphia Museum, The Encyclopedia of Greater Philadelphia – www.philadelphia-encyclopedia.org/essays/peales-

However, when the bears broke out and ate a monkey, then rampaged through Peale's house, he shot and ate them.

Bear meat was a new taste in the East, and plenty of people had a craving for the exotic. Food on the expeditions was usually a "catch-as-catch-can" proposition, so exploration parties became accustomed to new fare. The Lewis and Clark expedition consumed 190 dogs, to the extent that dog meat became the "favorite food"[93] of many members.

Pike was purportedly the first person of European descent to discover the roadrunner, although residents of Spanish New Mexico must have been familiar with it. The creature was unknown to science until 1829, but Pike trapped two of them in 1806 in the same cage on Christmas Day. One killed the other.

As new information emerged about Wilkinson's dealings with disgraced Vice President Burr, Pike was entangled in charges of being a party to treason rather than receiving the joyous welcome home he expected. Wilkinson had in his career committed everything from "petty chicanery to treason."[94] Washington Irving wrote of the "pompous, cocksure gallant"[95] Wilkinson that if he had not become a general, he would have made an "admirable trumpeter."[96] Still, despite his oath to a foreign power and his illegal pension, Wilkinson was able to repeatedly dupe Jefferson.

The scandal erupted over Pike's potential association with Wilkinson and Burr's treason even before he was released. Burr is now most notorious for his duel with Alexander Hamilton, but after he left office, he was accused of purchasing land in the West with the intent of establishing a separate empire. Wilkinson, it seems, had been under investigation since he arrived from Maryland as a young physician, and while Pike was not formally charged with treason, many labeled him a traitor, "a parasite of Wilkinson"[97] and "the beast of Santa Fe."[98] Some claimed that he was responsible for the murder of one of his men who had "threatened to reveal the true purposes of the Arkansas River Expedition."[99] His behavior after his return suggested that he was not the treasonous type, despite being "naïve, egotistical, and extremely ambitious."[100]

---

philadelphia-museum/

[93] Michael D. Wise

[94] Donald Jackson, American Heritage

[95] Donald Jackson, American Heritage

[96] Donald Jackson, American Heritage

[97] W.E. Hollon

[98] W.E. Hollon

[99] W.E. Hollon

[100] W.E. Hollon

Burr

Pike's strong link to Wilkinson required him to protest his innocence to Secretary of War Henry Dearborn, who absolved him of guilt entirely. Dearborn went on to laud the information Pike had brought back with him, despite not reaching the level of the Lewis and Clark expedition.

Dearborn

In a moment of quick thinking, Wilkinson changed the plan and left himself out of it. Spain controlled most of the Southwest and "resented the growing presence of trappers and mountain men the Purchase had brought in.[101] They suspected most of the trappers of being spies, and "there was some truth to this."[102] Information sharing was out of control, so Wilkinson did a turnabout and exposed Burr to Jefferson, making him appear to be a collaborator. A surprised Pike said that he assumed the information gathered was to be used by the U.S. in case of war against Spain. In one fell swoop, Wilkinson sent Pike to find the easiest southwestern routes for conquering the Spanish territories, then "betrayed Burr's idea to Thomas Jefferson, reached an agreement with the Spanish to neutralize the Texas frontier, placed New Orleans under martial law, and apprehended Burr."[103] This was all done in a deft diplomatic and political double-cross that left Wilkinson in good standing with both sides.

Some claim that Wilkinson gave up Burr because he wasn't allowed to be in charge of the

---

[101] W.E. Hollon

[102] Hill, Matthew, Zebulon Pike, Biography, Facts, and Timeline – www.study.com/academy/lesson/zebulon-pike-biography-facts-timeline.html

[103] Hill, Matthew

"operation." Wilkinson was known to live by the adage that it was "better to reign in Hell than to serve in Heaven."[104] Burr's scheme may have been of such a degree of audacity and magnitude as to scare Wilkinson off, especially with the number of people in on it, or he me simply might have become hesitant when Burr was twice arrested for his various scandals.

Wilkinson was without a doubt the mastermind behind the Pike expeditions, so one would assume there was more there than historically meets the eye. When he was paid for the fake invasion plan by the Spanish, there was Pike appearing in the vicinity as at least partial proof. In this way, he used Pike as "a willing or unwilling dupe."[105]

If Pike knew the real plan behind the plan, he was of the type to be tempted. He was an ambitious young officer who felt that the peacetime army left him little room for advancement and fame. He saw and heard the accolades being offered to Lewis and Clark, and he may have wanted to emulate them, even for nefarious reasons. Donald Jackson observed that "what Wilkinson was up to…has remained a mystery. It appears as though being in collaboration with Aaron Burr, he was planning a coup in the west."[106] It could have been a "traitorous moment"[107] designed to separate the western territories from the union or "a plot to conquer the Spanish borderlands without officially involving the United States,"[108] garnering the region for the U.S. and circumventing war with Spain. Either way, Pike's expedition served Wilkinson's needs, "official or unofficial."[109]

On the other hand, in every other facet of life, Pike seemed to be an avid patriot. W.E. Hollon, an authority on early, called Wilkinson "vain, bombastic, and incompetent, a master of petty treason with the gift of scandal."[110] According to Timothy Kibby, a close confidant of Wilkinson, "Lieutenant Pike was yet unaware of the nature of…the journey."[111] He suggested that even if Pike knew of the Spanish payments, he was "too good an officer to balk at the orders of his general."[112] Despite the suspect details of the expedition, Pike disavowed knowledge of anything untoward for the rest of his life.

Whatever the case, many facts Pike reported later were "for the great part very inaccurate."[113] He is reputed to have stolen a map made by Baron von Humboldt, a Prussian naturalist and explorer. Pike copied his map, used it, and published it later. It was the most advanced available

---

[104] Donald Jackson, American Heritage

[105] Encyclopedia.com

[106] Legends of America

[107] Legends of America

[108] Legends of America

[109] Legends of America

[110] Johnny D. Boggs, True West, Zebulon Pike's Life on the Mississippi – www.truewestmagazine.com/article/zebulon-pikes-life-on-the-mississippi/

[111] Monticello, Zebulon Pike

[112] Biography, Zebulon Pike

[113] Encyclopedia.com

for the time, but whatever the subtleties of the story, Pike was likely seriously lost on more than one occasion.

During the Wilkinson trial, Pike refused to say anything incriminating against his commander, and he "wrote passionate pleas in the General's defense."[114] It is likely that with Spain's economic burdens at home, the Southwest would eventually have been purchased anyway, but Pike's expedition did raise public awareness about the region, and as soon as he realized the availability of fur in the Southwest alone, he began to promote the value of the region.

Forced to clear his name without sinking the career of his superior officer, it was concluded by the courts and the military that Pike acted in the best interests of his country. He resumed his military career without interruption. Burr was charged with treason, but he was acquitted at a trial in which Wilkinson testified.

Although plenty of written evidence points to Wilkinson and Burr collaborating on a potentially treasonous project, it's still unclear to historians what the plan was or how far the scheme went. At the same time, suspicion of Pike has been kept alive "by the mystery surrounding his personal papers,"[115] for which a long fruitless search has been conducted through many decades. It may be that Wilkinson and Pike knew each other before the Louisiana Purchase was enacted since his father served under the general, and that Pike was fully aware of Wilkinson's allegiances.

While citing the possibilities of impropriety, Donald Jackson, who assembled what could be found of Pike's journals and letters, did not judge him harshly. He described Pike, for all his failures and extreme character traits, as "one of the most daring and adventuresome of the American explorers."[116] He added that the unofficial companion, Dr. Robinson, was likely not a conspirator, nor an emissary to the Spanish, but a "free-lance adventurer."[117]

There is one letter between Pike and Wilkinson that is telling, although it does not shed direct light on the Burr Conspiracy. The letter from the general contains instructions to Pike in the event of his capture, advising the expedition leader to be "circumspect and discrete…as you will be held responsible for consequences. If you discover that any tricks have been played, you will give me the names. Should fortune favor you…our country will, I think, make your future life comfortable."[118]

If Pike is to be considered as a willing tool of the nefarious Wilkinson and Burr conspiracy, it must be done largely by circumstantial evidence."[119] His association with Wilkinson was

---

[114] Encyclopedia.com

[115] W.E. Hollon, Oxford Journals

[116] Donald Jackson, Review by Harvey Carter, Colorado College

[117] Donald Jackson

[118] W.E. Hollon, the American Philosophical Society

[119] W.E. Hollon

accidentally brought about by the purchase of the Louisiana Territory and by his early attachment to the First Infantry Regiment at Kaskaskia, Illinois.

Dr. I.J. Cox, a well-known researcher of the Southwest, confirms that no presidential authorization was granted for his expeditions. It is not illogical to assume that Pike's second expedition was "designated to obtain information for the use of Burr and Wilkinson in their invasion of Mexico."[120]

However, sending a man disguised as a trader would have caused much less attention, although his return was almost entirely unheralded. The *National Intelligencer* of August 29, 1807, commented, "Captain Pike, who has been detained in the interior provinces of Spanish America arrived at this place, Nathitoches, in the evening of 30th last month. His friends and family were overjoyed to learn of his safe return."[121]

Jefferson discussed Pike's expeditions, in particular his meetings with the various tribes in 1808, in that year's message to the Senate. Pike and Jefferson exchanged letters late in 1807, but outside of a "faint-hearted" thank you for the bears, that was the extent of their correspondence. The two never met in person.

In the end, Pike was absolved of guilt by his contemporaries, but the academic community remains somewhat divided on Pike's possible "shadowy role"[122] in the Burr Conspiracy. Was he a spy for the Spanish like his commanding officer? Did he intend to provoke the Spanish into a conflict they were unlikely to win? Was he cooperating with a foreign power against his own country? No one has been able to take Pike's case past the circumstantial, and it may remain that way.

A Military Man

Pike was promoted to the rank of major in 1808, his career unfazed by earlier scandal, and in his accounts of the previous three years, he praised, albeit in a backhanded way, the men who had been with him through the years. Pike dubbed them with an odd nickname, writing, "For these men have served with me many a long year and notwithstanding they are such Dam'd Rascals that you keep no ducks or fowls for them, yet I think them very clever fellows – perfectly capable of getting the job done, but all in all, a set of Dam'd Rascals."[123]

Pike's *Account of Expeditions* was published in 1810 and translated into Dutch, German, and French due to its high popularity. In the following years, it became "compulsory"[124] reading for

[120] W.E. Hollon

[121] W.E. Hollon

[122] Robert McNamara

[123] Jimmy L. Bryan

[124] Interesting World Facts, 10 Interesting Facts about Zebulon Pike, Oct. 21, 2016 – www.interestingworldfacts.com/10-interesting-facts-about-zebulon-pike

19th century explorers, many of whom faithfully read his entire work.

Pike was appointed Battery Commander of the Army's Fourth Infantry Regiment, and a few months later in 1811, he fought at the Battle of Tippecanoe under future president William Henry Harrison, an Indianan originally from Virginia. The Battle of Tippecanoe was fought against a confederation led by the Shawnee on the banks of the Tippecanoe River in the heart of central Indiana. Earlier that year, Pike had been given command of U.S. troops stationed at Baton Rouge. So rigorous was his training regimen that they performed exceptionally well at Tippecanoe. Soon after, he was promoted to Lieutenant Colonel.

Lieutenant Colonel Pike fought again with the 4th Infantry in July 1812 and was promoted to lead the 15th Infantry in July. His duties included serving as Deputy Quartermaster-General in New Orleans and Inspector-General.

The War of 1812 is often overlooked in comparison to other conflicts in American history, but it was still an important one with many causes. Great Britain, as the leader of several coalitions of conservative European countries trying to isolate and snuff out the revolutionary spirit and the ambitions of Napoleon, had been at war with France almost continuously since 1792. Under President Thomas Jefferson (1801-1809) and James Madison (1809-1817), the United States tried to steer a course that would keep it from being drawn into the European war and defend its neutrality on the high seas. However, both Britain and France wanted to hurt the other side economically by keeping goods out of their enemy's hands. Thus, they did not faithfully respect the rights of neutral nations. The British government in 1807 had issued the "Orders in Council," which enforced a naval blockade against France, and with a shortage of seamen to man the Royal Navy, Britain also felt justified in stopping and sometimes firing on ships flying the American flag in the name of apprehending escaped British sailors.

The other main cause of war was distress on the Northwestern frontier, where the British in Canada were supporting Indian resistance to American settlement. So-called "War Hawks" from that region in Congress pushed for a declaration of war. Some hoped that a war would not only stop Indian depredations but evict the British from Canada and lead to completion of some unfinished business from the American Revolution, namely Canada joining the U.S.

As the historian Robert V. Rimini has pointed out, there was another unspoken motive for the U.S. to declare war on Great Britain. A need was felt to show Great Britain and the other countries of the Old World that the new republic in North America was not something to be trifled with, and that henceforth it needed to be taken seriously. While the Federalist Party with its stronghold in New England was pro-British, the ruling Democratic-Republican Party tilted towards France, and after a long build-up, President Madison asked Congress for a declaration of war against Great Britain, which a heavily divided Congress passed on June 18, 1812. Unknown to them because of the time it took for a ship with news to cross the ocean, the British government ended up repealing the "Orders in Council" on June 23, 1812.

It's ironic that a battle in New Orleans would be the most famous battle of the war because most of the War of 1812 was fought over and around the U.S.-Canadian border. The fighting there was fought on three different fronts: near Detroit, around Niagara and Buffalo, and between upstate New York and Lower Canada (Quebec). There was also fighting involving British and Atlantic ships on the Great Lakes and in the Atlantic, where the Royal Navy imposed a blockade of American ports south of New England (whose opposition to the war the British wished to encourage).

When the war began, Pike was promoted to full Colonel, leading the 15th Regiment stationed on Lake Champlain, on the border between New York and Vermont. As the leader of the military effort, Dearborn decided in consultation with others that the U.S. should attack Montreal, among Canada's most well-defended and most important cities, but as Pike's 600 men waited along the shores of Lake Champlain in Plattsburg, New York, the plan was abandoned.

Pike received permission to enter Canada for small actions on November 21, 1812 with his regiment. They met and scattered small groups of Canadian soldiers and native warriors during their campaign, and Pike had the enemy camps burned before heading back to the U.S. border. On the way, a skirmish ensued that turned out to be against another U.S. force. Two were killed, with three wounded.

Among the first engagements of the war, Pike commanded the advance guard of the American force that was defeated at the Battle of Lacolle Mills in November of 1812. The defeat was laid at the feet of Dearborn for his poor planning and halfhearted effort.

In the spring of 1813, the plan to invade Canada changed shape. Now it was to proceed through the cities of Kingston and York (modern Toronto), both major shipbuilding centers. Too ill to command the attack on York himself, Dearborn assigned the duty to Pike, who had been promoted to Brigadier General only a few months before. The promotion was accelerated when several openings appeared. Some disarray was evident in the higher echelons as General William Eustis was removed as Secretary of War.

Since he was already famous as an explorer, Pike's new recruits were sent to Staten Island, New York with great anticipation, and Pike expected to join them soon. He was once again under the command of Wilkinson, who so "ineptly commanded the American forces…that another court martial ended his military career."[125] In a letter to Wilkinson, Pike wrote "If we go to Canada, you will hear of my fame or of my death – for I am determined to seek the 'Bubble' even in the cannon's mouth."[126] He continued to dream of a hero's death.

After less than a week's training in Staten Island, Pike's regiment was transported up the Hudson, and they joined a force of about 6,000 men to march toward the Canadian border. Along

---

[125] W.E. Hollon, Pike and the York Campaign
[126] W.E. Hollon

with General Jacob Brown, Pike departed from the newly fortified rural military outpost of Sacket Harbor on the New York side of Lake Ontario.

Pike led 1,700 troops onto the ships of Commander Isaac Chauncey, and among his first orders was an edict against looting in case of victory. All personal property of the enemy was to be respected, with no theft to be tolerated, regardless of how slight. He boarded the *Madison*, from which he would direct the landing.

A company of riflemen was the first unit to attack the British, and as he grew impatient with rifle fire and shore batteries preventing the landing of American troops, Pike personally took command. According to accounts from those on the ship, he turned to his aide and shouted, "By God, I can't stand here any longer. Come on, jump in my boat!"[127] His arrival on shore was likely a premature decision.

Pike was one of the first ashore, urging on his men, and many of the native contingents opposing the AMericans "were now utterly demoralized, shouting, "Too many Yankee!"[128] They threw down their arms and fled in all directions. After a few shots from the riflemen, the British began to fall back. Pike pursued, burning their blockhouses and barracks as he went.

Battle of York by Owen Staples

British General Roger Hale Sheaffe soon raised the white flag, realizing that the city would be lost, and he drew the soldiers back into the fort for a retreat to Kingston. As the British retreated, they destroyed their military equipment to keep them out of enemy hands.

A group of Pike's men were sent forward to seek a formal surrender as Pike helped an injured man to the rear. A soldier approached with a British prisoner and asked his commander if he would like to question him. Before Pike could answer, "a terrible explosion rent the air."[129] The

---

[127] Biography, Zebulon Pike
[128] W.E. Hollon
[129] W.E. Hollon

British had destroyed one of their own ammunition stores, and a piece of the stone shrapnel hit Pike square in the back. He lay prone and exclaimed that his wound felt mortal. It was found that the stone "had torn a great hole in his back."[130] American casualties numbered 52 dead from the explosion, with 180 wounded.

When hit, Pike passed on command to Colonel Cromwell Pearce and purportedly said, "Push on my brave fellows and avenge your general."[131] Amid the disorder and lack of strong leadership following the battle, American troops forgot Pike's order about looting and went on a rampage through the town of York, looting and burning public buildings. The riot was ignited by the discovery of a scalp in one of the government offices, fueling a belief that the British were paying natives for the scalps of American citizens.

Pike was carried back to the *Madison*, where he died on April 27, 1813. His troops went on to capture the town and place the British flag behind his head just before he breathed his last. The 34-year-old explorer and general "lived long enough to hear the cheers of his men."[132]

Pike had written to his father before the battle and "seemed to anticipate"[133] that he might not survive it, in addition to citing the honorable mention he would receive. A quotation of the letter can be found in John K. Mahon's *The War of 1812*: "If success attends my steps, honor and glory await my name – if defeat, still it should be said we died like brave men and conferred honor, even in death, on the American name."[134]

In part, Pike today is overlooked much the same way the War of 1812 is, and Mahon poignantly explained one of the reasons why that was the case: "The War of 1812 is a perfect example of how a war should not be conducted."[135] Congress failed to supply sufficient revenue to support an ill-equipped, poorly trained militia – "little effective coordination of the war from Washington."[136] Americans were deeply divided over the war, and many states "failed to mobilize their militias when directed to by the government,"[137] declaring the federal call to arms as unconstitutional.

Zebulon Montgomery Pike was buried in a hero's funeral at the military cemetery of Sackets Harbor in New York. The USS *General Pike* was launched two months after his death.

Pike may have hoped that military exploits would further propel his legacy, and he may have been officially cleared in all the investigations surrounding Burr and Wilkinson, but it seems his

---

[130] W.E. Hollon

[131] Encyclopedia.com

[132] Biography Zebulon Pike

[133] Encyclopedia.com

[134] Encyclopedia.com

[135] John K. Mahon - www.books.org/books/the-war-of-1812/john-k-mahon/9780306804298

[136] John K. Mahon

[137] John K. Mahon

reputation couldn't fully avoid the taint. Congress had refused to grant Pike funds to compensate him for his "interrupted journey of discovery"[138] before he died in the American assault on York, and for plenty of historians and biographers, Pike's relative insignificance today is one of the main themes of his story. John Logan Allen of the University of Wyoming noted somewhat sardonically that it was Pike's mistakes that made him important. Many mistakes and errant calculations of waterways got into the next generation of maps, and accomplishments are so often in this way qualified.

Much is made of how Pike "died with his boots on"[139] and how men bravely followed him anywhere he asked them to go. While this is true, it is worth noting that he overtly threatened his men with death for any mutinous talk or action, so there was also plenty of peril for anyone who did not follow him.

Some suggest that Pike was on a path to become president at some point, such was the fervor induced by his actions. This speculation is obviously a moot point, but it seems plausible considering his valor in the last battle of his life.

Since his death, Pike has been memorialized with ships, counties, dams, and lakes, islands, parks, and towns. His memory faded somewhat following the Civil War, but there was a resurgence in 1906, the centennial of his Southwest expedition. In 1901, General William Jackson Palmer honored Pike with a statue in Colorado Springs. The Pike National Forest is also located in Colorado. Fort Pike stands in New Orleans, and Camp Pike is located in Arkansas. Likewise, the Pike National Historic Trail Association was created in 2007 "to promote and preserve his legacy."[140]

People in the 20th century focused mostly on his exploration, while those in the 19th century worked with his maps. Pike, among others, "probed the American interiors with the mindset of surveyors and policy agents who fashioned meticulous geographies of the physical world,"[141] although he was far from the most elegant mapmakers. The maps of early America served as "charts that reflected the transcontinental destiny of the country. Maps became monuments to American nationalism."[142]

Maps constructed during the time of Jefferson's presidency seemed impervious to "fancifulness exhibited in novels, poetry, and landscape art,"[143] even though they were of varying qualities. Pike published five maps in *Account of Expeditions*. He produced credibly accurate delineations of river courses, mountain ranges, native and Spanish communities, and

---

[138] Matthew Harris, Jay H. Buckley

[139] Matthew Harris, Jay H. Buckley

[140] Zebulon Pike, Zebulon Montgomery Pike Expeditions and Life/Legacy – www.zebulonpike.org

[141] Jimmy L. Bryan, Unquestionable Geographies, *Pacific Historical Review*, Fall 2018, Vol.; 87 No. 4

[142] Jimmy L. Bryan

[143] Jimmy L. Bryan

paths of their expeditions. His map displayed the Arkansas River and its "highest peak." The name of Pikes Peak was added to the mountain decades after Pike's death, but trappers and early settlers had begun calling it by his name years before.

American citizens had become "sophisticated readers of maps"[144] by the early 19th century, and for those living in the days of early westward exploration, maps conveyed emotion. "The revolutionary generation had achieved a 'geographical literacy' not only to measure and document the continent, but also awakening an exceptionalist sentiment."[145] America was a "geographical distinction before it was defined as a community or nation."[146] Maps bound "America" as a place with "Americans" as a people.[147] Journeys "were at once scientific and ethnographic in nature…but also coupled with explicit objectives expanding United States commerce and extending the nation's authority."[148]

Biographers have faced obvious challenges since Pike's expeditions are controversial and less meticulous than the work produced by Lewis and Clark, not to mention the fact Pike's death and lack of personal papers left permanent gaps in the record. As a result, historians are "remarkably varied"[149] in their evaluations of Pike, who has been labeled a "lost explorer, a spy, a co-conspirator of Aaron Burr and a hero of the republic."[150]

Of all the side-effects of the expeditions and his career in general, one overlooked aspect is the excitement he created in the conscience of the American public over Texas, helping to spur the expansionist movement and the urge to settle there before it became a U.S. territory.

Eventually, Donald Jackson presented an updated version of Pike's journals in two volumes with captured maps and papers that lay in Mexico for nearly a century. To him, Pike's affiliation with Burr "fades from lack of evidence,"[151] and his loyalty to Wilkinson was "more boyish than sinister."[152] Jackson asserted that Pike was simply dogged by bad luck, further noting that when he tried to turn his *Account of Expeditions* into royalties, the publisher went bankrupt.

Ultimately, Jackson lamented Pike's "near misses" in life and death, even if those near misses made sense: "Nothing Zebulon Montgomery Pike ever tried to do was easy…"[153]

---

[144] Jimmy L. Bryan

[145] Jimmy L. Bryan

[146] Jimmy L. Bryan

[147] Jimmy L. Bryan

[148] Susan Gaunt Stearns

[149] Matthew Harris, Jay H. Buckley, Review by Susan Gaunt Stearns, *The Journal of Southern History*, Aug. 2013, Vol. 79 no.3

[150] Susan Gaunt Stearns

[151] Harris, Matthew, Buckley, Jay H., Review by Susan Gaunt Stearns

[152] Harris, Matthew, Buckley, Jay H., Review by Susan Gaunt Stearns

[153] Harris, Matthew, Buckley, Jay H., Review by Susan Gaunt Stearns

Online Resources

Other books about 19th century American history by Charles River Editors

Other books about Pike on Amazon

Further Reading

Biography. Zebulon Pike, Your Dictionary – www.biography.yourdictionary.com/zebulon-pike

Boggs, Johnny, True West, Zebulon Pike's Life on the Mississippi – www.truewestmagazine.com/article/zebulon-pikes-life-on-the-mississippi/

Britannica, James Wilkinson – www.britannica.com/biography/James-Wilkinson

Bryan. Jimmy L., Unquestionable Geographies, *Pacific Historical Review*, Fall 2018, Vol.; 87 No. 4

Carter, Carroll Joe, Pike in Colorado, Review by Maxine Benson, Adams State College, Alamosa

Celebnetworth, Biography and Timeline, Zebulon Montgomery Pike – www.celebnetworth.comZebulon-Pike

Cutrer, Thomas, TSHA, Texas State Historical Association, Pike, Zebulon Montgomery (1799-1813) – www.tshaonline.org/handbook/entries/pike-zebulon-montgomery

Dedicated Writers, Biography – www.dedicatedwriters.com/biographies/Zebulon-Pike-34961.htm

Encyclopedia.com, Zebulon Montgomery Pike www.encyclopedia.com

Hill, Matthew, Zebulon Pike, Biography, Facts, and Timeline – www.study.com/academy/lesson/zebulon-pike-biography-facts-timeline.html

History, This Day in History, April 27, 1813 – www.history.com/this-day-in-history/explorer-zebulon-pike-dies

Hollon, W.E., Oxford Journals, Zebulon Pike's Lost Papers, *The Mississippi Valley Historical Review*, Sept. 1947, Vol. 34 No. 2

Hollon, W.E., Zebulon Montgomery Pike and the Wilkinson-Burr Conspiracy, Proceedings of the *American Philosophical Society*, Dec. 3, 1947, Vol. 91, no. 5

Hollon, W.E., Zebulon M. Pike and the New York Campaign, 1813 – *New York History*, Vol.

30 no. 3 (July 1949) Cornell University

Harris, Matthew, Buckley, Jay H., Review by Susan Gaunt Stearns, Thomas Jefferson and the Opening of the American West, *The Journal of Southern History*, Aug. 2013, Vol. 79 No. 3

Harris, Matthew, Buckley, Jay H., Review by Adan Jortner, Thomas Jefferson and the Opening of the American West, *Journal of the Early Republic* Vol. 33 No. 1 (Spring 2013)

History of Pike's Peak – www.pikespeak.us.com/learn-history-of-pikes-peak

Indiana Historical Society, We Do History, June 8, 1796 – www.images.indianahistory.org/digital/collection/id/1658/

Interesting World Facts, 10 Interesting Facts about Zebulon Pike, Oct. 21, 2016 – www.interestingworldfacts.com/10-interesting-facts-about-zebulon-pike[154]

Jackson Donald, Pathfinder's Papers, Zebulon Montgomery Pike Review by Robert F. Aethern, Minnesota History Vol. 40 No. 3 (Fall 1966)

Jackson, Donald, The Journals of Zebulon Montgomery Pike: With Letters and Related Documents, Review by Harvey L. Carter, Colorado College

Jackson, Donald, *American Heritage Foundation*, The Question Is: How Lost Was Zebulon Pike? Feb. 1965, Vol. 16 No. 2

Legends of America, Zebulon Pike, Hard-Luck Soldier & Explorer – www.legendsofamerica.com/we-zebulonpike/

Kit Morgan Benson, Zebulon Montgomery Pike, biography – www.findagrave.com/memorial/815/Zebulon-montgomery-pike

Mahon, John K., The War of 1812, Books.org – www.books.org/books/the-war-of-1812/john-k-mahon/97803068042981/

McNamara, Robert, Zebulon Pike's Mysterious Western Expeditions, Mysterious Motives Remain Puzzling to This Day, Thought Com 2/2/2019 – www.thoughtco.com/zebulon-pike-led-two-expeditions-1773817

Midwestern Weekends, Pike on the Prowl, For Better or Worse, America's First Emissary on the Upper Mississippi Set History into Motion, Dec. 1, 2020 – www.midwesternweekends.com/plan-a-trip/history-heritage/frontier-history/zebulon-pike/

Monticello, Zebulon Pike – www.monticello.org/research-education/thomas-jefferson-encyclopedia/zebulon-pike/

Nebraska Studies, Zebulon Pike – www.nebraskastudies.org/en/1800-1849/the-louisiana-purchase/zebulon-pike/

Oklahoma Historical Society, The Encyclopedia of Oklahoma History and Culture, Pike-Wilkinson Expeditions – www.history.org/publications/enc.entry?entry=P1007

Orsi, Jared, Zebulon Pike, Colorado Encyclopedia – www.coloradoencyclopedia.org/article/zebulon-montgomery-pike

Orsi, Jared, Book Reviews, The Life of Zebulon Pike, Review by Stephen Aaron, *Book Reviews*, UCLA

Orsi, Jared, The Life of Zebulon Pike, Review by Marcus Soli, *Journal of American History* Vol. 101 No. 3 (Dec., 2014)

Orsi, Jared, Citizen Explorer, Review by Barton H. Barbain, *Pacific Historical Review*, Vol. 85 No. 1 (Feb 2016)

Orsi, Jared, Zebulon Pike and his "Frozen Lands, Bodies, Nationalism, and the West in the Early Republic, *Western Historical Quarterly* Vol. 42 No. 1 (Spring 2011)

Our Iowa Heritage, Zebulon Pike and His Dam'd Rascals – www.ouriowaheritagew.com/our-iowa-heritage-zebulon-pike

Santa Fe Trail Research, Zebulon Pike's Expedition to the Southwest-1807 – www.santafetrailresearch.com/pike/expedition.html

Soli, Marco, When the Mississippi Was an Indian River, University of Michigan, *Revue français d'études américaine*, Dec. 2003, No. 98, Stemming the Mississippi

Sweeney, Kevin Z., Wither the Fruited Plain: The Long Expedition and the Description of the "Great American Desert," *Great Plains Quarterly* Vol. 25 No. 2 (Spring 2005), University of Nebraska

The US-Dakota War of 1862, Lieutenant Zebulon Pike - www.usdakotawar.org/history/lieutenant-zebulon-pike

When America Was Young, Zebulon Pike and the Santa Fe Trail – www.whenamericawasyoung.com/pike-santa-fe-trail[155]

---

[155] When America Was Young, Zebulon Pike and the Santa Fe Trail – www.whenamericawasyoung.com/pike-santa-fe-trail

Wise, Michael D., Seeing Like a Stomach: Food, the Body, and Jeffersonian Exploration in the Near Southwest, *Southwestern Historical Quarterly* Vol. 120 No. 4 (April 2017)

World History, US, Zebulon Pike to Santa Fe, July 4, 2017 – www.worldhistory.org/american-history/the-grat-american-plains/zebulon-pike-to-santa-fe.php

Zebulon Pike, America's Mountain is Pike's Peak – www.zebulonpike.org/americas-mountain-is-pikes-peak/

Zebulon Pike, Zebulon Montgomery Pike Expeditions and Life/Legacy – www.zebulonpike.org

Zebulon Pike, the Pike-Zebulon Tradition – www.zebulonpike.org/the-pike-zebulon-tradition/